Fireplace
ideas

contents

The data given in this book is used to exemplify typical installations. Since specifications are subject to change, please write to The Majestic Company, Huntington, Indiana 46750, for the latest product literature. Majestic will not assume responsibility for faulty or unsafe fireplace installations where equipment has not been installed according to the instructions given.

the lasting joys of the fireside....

Fads and fashions in home building come and go, but one thing never changes, and that is the home owner's desire for the nostalgic, heart-warming pleasures of a blazing log fire.

From the old-time stone hearth to the ultra-modern, free-standing model, the fireplace remains the decorative focal point and provides much of the warmth and cheer in today's homes. Just as in a lovable antique or a family heirloom, people find that here is a household feature out of the past that is well worth preserving.

In fact, it has been found that practically everyone engaged in building a new home or remodeling an old one either wants, or is actually planning to include, some type of fireplace.

With your interest in fireplaces in mind, we of The Majestic Company are pleased to welcome you to the pages of this book and to share with you our many years of experience in fireplace construction and the making of related components. Our intention is to bring you the greatest possible satisfaction and enjoyment from your fireplace installation, whichever type you may choose.

from raw necessity to gracious refinement...

Since early man first needed a "place for fire" to warm himself and cook his food, the fireplace has come a long way in its evolution to an eye-appealing and comfort-giving home feature.

Even in the hut, which came thousands of years after the prehistoric cave, a simple hole in the roof was often the only means of emitting the smoke from the fire that blazed or smoldered in the center of indoor human activity.

In many cases, even in more elaborate later dwellings such as medieval baronial halls, a central hearth, without sides, held a blazing fire with no actual smoke opening. The smoke merely rose, accumulating in the high ceiling areas, and eventually found its way outdoors through chinks in the construction.

An early dwelling with a simple hole in the roof

Gradually, those with an engineering turn of mind developed more complex devices to burn and control the fire which meant so much to human survival and progress. They trended away from the central hearth and towards an enclosed firebox and channeled opening (chimney) to direct the smoke upward and outward.

Primitive dome-shaped fireplaces of adobe reflect this early inventiveness. Soil with a high clay content was mixed with water, sand, grass (and later lime) to form the crude, curving fireboxes and flues found among the remains of Indian and other early civilizations.

A primitive shaped fireplace

Field stones were later used. They were "puddled" or set in a mortar-like clay mixture. Bricks, first introduced into America around the end of the 18th Century, assumed several shapes, sizes and modes of decoration and have lasted through the centuries as a popular fireplace material.

Since early fireplaces were the only source of warmth in the home, they were necessarily large and space-consuming. There remain in America's earliest homes some fine examples of the massive, all-purpose brick or stone bases that included, from basement to roof-top, all types of storage spaces, multiple fireplaces, dutch ovens and meat smoking rooms, not to mention the flues necessary to carry away the smoke. An archway was often built through the base at the cellar floor level, with storage areas and shelves designed into the interior of the arch.

In early times, when wood was plentiful, fireplaces were large enough to burn logs six to eight feet in length, and smoke rooms accommodated whole pigs and other animals without slicing or quartering. Smoke houses, apart from the dwelling, were also in wide use.

Needless to say, without the fireplace there was no home. The fireplace was often built with an "ingle nook" big enough for a chair and a member of the family such as an older or ailing person in need of

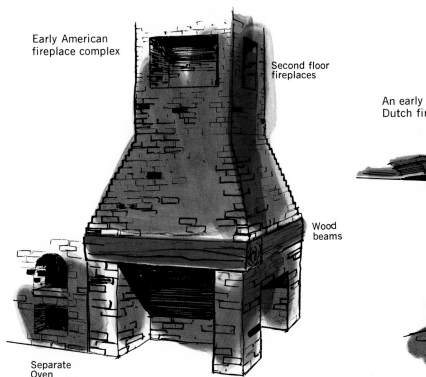

Early American
fireplace complex

Second floor
fireplaces

Wood
beams

Separate
Oven

An early
Dutch fireplace

extra warmth and comfort. Never to be forgotten are the heavy iron crane and pot which hung in the huge fireplace and filled the family's cooking needs. Bread and meat were usually baked or roasted in ovens adjacent to, or built into, the actual firebox portion. Sometimes these ovens were high enough to avoid the actual flames so that wood doors could be used. Others had no doors at all, and still others had iron doors. Some of the ovens were connected to the main fireplace flue. Others were separate and had their own "ash ovens" below as individual sources of heat. The centrally-located complex of fireplaces, ovens, storage spaces and smoke rooms took many variations, and one seldom found two constructions exactly alike.

As the brick stack ascended, it accommodated still other fireplace flues from bedrooms on upper floors. The massive brick stack containing multiple flues became a commonplace.

Fireplaces became extremely elaborate in design and ornamentation as shown in some of the fanciful European and American styles sketched on these pages from photos of restorations.

(One can only imagine the inefficiency of the early fireplace. Ben Franklin, who contributed much to the development of early home heating devices, wrote that the fireplaces of his day sent all but one sixth of their heat up the chimney.)

As wood became less plentiful, fireplaces became smaller, and as other means of cooking and central heating came into regular use, the fireplace took on

the aspects of an entertainment center, a rallying spot where members of the family and their friends gathered for relaxation, refreshment and conviviality.

Though most fireplaces of today are smaller and more manageable than their ancient forebears, the traditions of fellowship, warmth and cheer still surround the hearth with the open fire. Whatever the design treatment — whatever tastes the home owner may have in fireplaces — most will readily agree that Man really started something when he struck and fed fuel to the first mysterious blaze.

An Early American Type

what a modern fireplace is...
what it does

Though millions enjoy the warmth and friendly glow of an open fire, there are actually many persons who know little about the workings of a fireplace. How is it built? What are its parts? What happens to the air, fuel, flames and smoke that constitute a fire? These are a few of the questions to be answered.

First of all, any dictionary will define a fireplace, roughly, as a "wall recess, connected to an outlet (chimney), designed for the purpose of containing and encouraging an open fire." However, for the fireplace to look attractive and operate properly, more explanation is needed. The picture on this page shows the location of the basic parts of a typical fireplace construction. This and the accompanying glossary should give the reader a better understanding of the fireplace and its operation.

The Basic Principle

"Warm air rises" is a good beginning premise, but many other factors influence a fire! When the first flame leaps to life, a current of air is started in a generally upward direction. As the fuel is consumed, cooler air is drawn in around it, through the firebox opening, to supply additional oxygen for burning. The fire grows larger, and, as the smoke chamber and flue are heated, the heated surfaces increase the upward pull of the warm air and smoke. This pull is augmented by draft created by air moving across the top of the open chimney and by additional air entering the firebox opening.

Smoke, meanwhile, enters the smoke chamber and begins to eddy, especially in the early stages of the fire. This is caused by a certain amount of downdraft and a flue that is still relatively unheated and too cool to draw air upward. Before the days of smoke shelves and dampers, fireplaces burned inefficiently; the answer was usually a broad flue and a hot fire to minimize smoking.

The downdraft shelf in a properly built, modern fireplace traps smoke and keeps it from being blown back into the firebox by flue downdraft. This gives smoke a chance to swirl into the upward-moving, warmer stream of air created by the fire.

As the fire progresses, this heat stream becomes intensified. Although some of the heat goes up the flue with the smoke, even in the best-built fireplaces, there is considerable warming of the room by "convection" currents as air near the firebox tends to circulate. The greatest room-warming action, however, is by radiation, as heat rays emanate directly from the flames and embers and bounce off the back and sides of the firebox.

The combustion process itself is simple, but certain elements of construction, discovered by fireplace specialists working and experimenting through the ages, are essential to operational success. These elements will be discussed on later pages. Meanwhile, the following glossary of basic terms will help in the understanding of fireplace operation and serve as an aid in reading later sections of the book.

The Basic Parts

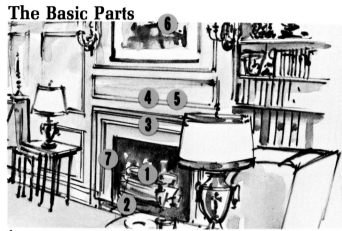

1. FIREBOX

The chamber which contains the fire. Usually constructed of firebrick, with the sides splayed outward and the upper portion of the back sloped forward to reflect maximum heat into the room.

2. HEARTH

This is the bottom of the firebox, or the area on which the fire is built. It should be of firebrick or other fireproof material. Its extension into the room is called the *Extended Hearth*.

3. THROAT

The opening, or the passageway, from the firebox to the smoke chamber. Located forward of the center of the firebox by virtue of a slanted rear firebox wall.

4. SMOKE CHAMBER

The space extending from the top of the throat, up to the bottom of the flue, and between the side walls. Generally triangular in shape, it serves to funnel the smoke into the smaller area of the flue opening.

5. SMOKE SHELF

A horizontal shelf as wide as the throat and extending backward from the rear of the throat to the rear flue wall. It diverts downdrafts and causes them to eddy and drift upward into the rising air currents.

6. FLUE

A vent or hollow stack that carries the products of combustion out of the house. Its size governs the volume of smoke it can handle; its height determines the production of draft.

7. SURROUND

Area immediately adjacent to top and sides of firebox opening. Always composed of non-combustible material such as brick, stone, marble, tile, glass, etc.

These are the very basic parts. Dampers and other mechanical components and refinements will be described on later pages.

the matter of style....
(and its influence)

The Spanish influence

Everyone has "taste"—and the outward appearance and mood of your fireplace will be of utmost importance to you. Its *style* will be reflected in the size and shape of the firebox opening, the mantel (if any), the hearth (raised or floor-level), and the material, treatment and color of surround and trim.

When style is mentioned, those who are decorator-conscious think of the terms "traditional" and "modern." Though few styles created today are pure "anything," it is possible to come close in designing a French Provincial, Georgian, Federal, Victorian, Modern or other style of fireplace to go with your chosen home and its furnishings. Combinations of different styles have been made with pleasing results. You can copy, or adapt from memory, any style you like. Ultimately, *you* must decide the style since you will *live* with the fireplace.

If you do not like any of the styles you have seen in pictures or in the homes of friends, do as many creative-minded persons do and make up your own. On succeeding pages you will see a broad variety of styles. Choose one, or let your imagination be your guide. The sky is the limit in planning the outward appearance, as long as the interior components and materials measure up to the standards necessary for safety and correct operation. If you wish to pursue "style" to the Nth degree, an architect or an interior decorator can be of invaluable assistance.

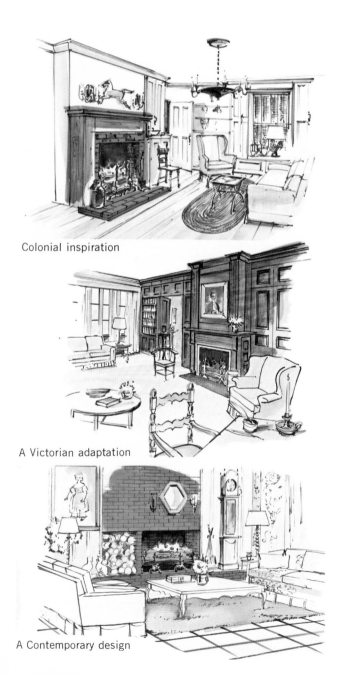

Colonial inspiration

A Victorian adaptation

A Contemporary design

An Italian
Renaissance
Fireplace

shape, material, treatment and color
establish the character of your fireplace

Combination wood paneling and white brick. Plank mantel.

Black glass surround—or metal with porcelain or fire resistant finish.

Rough stone surround. Cantilevered hearth, set with small tiles.

Brick surround. Wood paneling. Marble or slate hearth.

Raised firebox in formal brick. Stone or brick hearth at floor level.

Rough concrete surround and hearth. Wood paneling.

choose location

for Convenience and Frequency of Use

Living rooms and family rooms are the most common fireplace locations, though dining rooms and bedrooms are also frequent choices. Above all, put this important feature of the home in a *prominent place*, not in a seldom used room or corner.

Outside walls, where footings are most practical to build, are the usual locations, but many custom-built homes have the fireplace centrally located for maximum visual and entertainment advantage.

Multiple fireplaces, as well as multiple-opening single fireplaces, are discussed in later pages. Certain construction limitations, as well as your individual preference, will govern the placement.

Why put off the pleasures of a genuine wood-burning fireplace when you can enjoy them **now?** See your nearest Majestic dealer about one of the types of fireplaces described in this book. Ask your builder to put a fireplace in your new home. In most remodeling projects, a home-improvement loan provides easy financing.

Following are additional general pointers on fireplace construction before delving into specific types of fireplaces for your consideration and selection.

Safety

Always consult local building codes before building any kind of fireplace. Some codes do not permit certain types of fireplace construction. Should local codes be ignored and fire result, you may be in trouble with local authorities, as well as your insurance company.

Construction

Pay strict attention to basic construction rules given here and elsewhere. If a fireplace is not carefully built, it may develop smoke leaks and serious structural faults. Poor operation and home damage are the possible consequences.

Draft

Construction must adhere to thermo-dynamic standards worked out by combustion engineers to be sure of adequate draft. Consult the chart on Page 62 giving size relationships of firebox opening, flue, etc.

DO check the record and reputation of the firm or individual you hire for the job. Ask other homeowners if the fireplaces he built for them are successful!

DO plan ahead and be satisfied you have made the right decisions on details of construction. Mistakes, especially in heavy masonry, are difficult and expensive to repair.

DO construct all masonry so it will be self-supporting. A masonry fireplace and chimney should give no structural support to the house and should receive none from it.

DON'T install combustible finish and trim material closer than 6″ to the opening of your fireplace firebox.

DON'T complete your fireplace without giving it a thorough smoke test.

DON'T build a roaring fire in your masonry fireplace right after it is finished. Allow two to three weeks to elapse for seasoning of mortar. Otherwise serious cracks may develop.

Consider a Pre-Built

Want to forget all about proportioning? The pre-built, all-metal fireplace described on later pages is *pre-proportioned* and factory-built. Merely frame it in around wood studding and joists. Masonry may be used as finish material, though it is not needed. Much of the charm of a complete masonry fireplace results *without* the expense, inconvenience, and labor of full masonry construction. Heavy footers and much of the weight are eliminated.

How About More Than One?

If you are thinking of a back-to-back or an upstairs-downstairs combination of two fireplaces, you might do well to consider using pre-formed Majestic Circulator units, described on Page 74, or the Majestic Thulman Fireplace on Page 24.

These labor-saving fireplaces are a truly economical way to lessen the cost of building in and enjoying a real fireplace. (Placement of multiple fireplaces is diagramed on Page 27 and 75.)

Looking for Something Really Different?

Many of the fireplace types described in this book are adaptable to ultra-modern, even extreme, treatments. As long as the basic rules of construction and size-proportioning are obeyed, there is no limit to the extent of "customizing" you may do in building your own, truly individualized, fireplace. If additional answers are needed, write Majestic — or consult a local architect, contractor or fireplace specialist.

some typical questions and answers.....

Q. Why should I have an "old-fashioned" feature like a fireplace in my home?

A. A fireplace not only provides a charming, cheerful entertainment center, but also affords emergency warmth in case a power supply shut-off should interrupt the operation of your central heating system.

Q. How much does a fireplace cost?

A. Costs vary according to geographical location, materials used, and the size and complexity of your planned construction. They may run from a few hundred to thousands of dollars. Pre-built, pre-formed units are the most economical types of fireplace installation. In any case, if some or all of the work can be done by a "handyman" member of the family, costs will naturally be lowered.

Q. Must every fireplace have a deep footing of concrete?

A. In the case of a full-masonry fireplace, the answer is yes. In the case of the modern, all-metal, pre-built fireplace (see page 24), the answer is no. The latter type of fireplace is designed for placement directly on sub-flooring and against other wood surfaces with absolute safety.

Q. What are some simple "rules of thumb" to use in proportioning the various fireplace dimensions?

A. The various openings should be sized as follows:
Firebox height = 2/3 to 3/4 width
Firebox depth = 1/2 to 2/3 height
Throat opening = 1/5 to 1/4 firebox opening
Flue opening = 1/10 firebox opening

Q. How do you "cure" a smoky fireplace?

A. First, be sure the smoke passage from the open damper throat to the chimney top opening is absolutely clear.

A second remedy for fireplaces that smoke only slightly is the use of a fine mesh firescreen to reduce the air intake of the fireplace.

Since most smoking problems are a result of the flue being too small for the size of the firebox, a simple answer is the installation of a metal plate or canopy along the top of the firebox opening. Another is the reduction of the firebox size by adding interior layers of firebrick.

Another common cause is excessive downdraft produced by nearby buildings, trees or hills — or by a chimney located too far below the roof peak. Extension of chimney height or capping may stop the smoking (See Page 63).

Q. What is the easiest and least expensive fireplace to build?

A. In the Majestic Company's long experience with wood-burning fireplaces, there has never been a fireplace to equal the ease of construction and low cost of the pre-built, all-in-one fireplace which is fully described on Pages 15 through 36. Gas-fired fireplaces should also be taken into consideration, as described on Pages 38 and 39.

the art of building a fire

Selecting Fuel:

Real wood logs are generally most acceptable for use in an open fireplace, though some home owners may prefer, on occasion, to use coal or charcoal. At any rate, a wood fire is usually required to start other fuels, so the following pointers will apply in most cases.

Logs may be split or whole and should be 16″ to 22″ in length.

Dry, seasoned hardwoods, such as hickory, oak, walnut or most available fruitwoods, make the best fuel. Soft woods burn away too quickly; wet, green woods should be avoided because they smolder instead of burning clean.

Also avoid the use of scrap lumber or refuse. This material, especially when excessively dry, produces a great many sparks which escape up the flue and become a fire hazard.

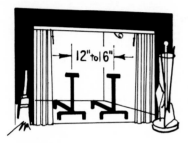

Setting the Fire:

If andirons are used, place them about 12″ to 16″ apart, equidistant from the center-line of the hearth. Lay a generous amount of crumpled or twisted newspaper on the hearth between the andirons, leaving a few convenient loose ends for igniting. Arrange a criss-cross of kindling sticks, such as pine, on the paper. (If a fire basket is used, this starting fire may be placed in or under the basket, allowing good air space.)

Set the longest and thickest of the logs (4″ or 5″ diameter) across the andirons and toward the back of the fireplace. (Not tight against the back. Leave about a ½″ space.) Place a second piece, preferably a split log, a few inches in front, then another split log on top, forming a pyramid.

Be Sure the Fireplace Damper is Open!

Before lighting the kindling, lay about a half-sheet of newspaper on the logs and set fire to it. This warms the flue and establishes a draft. While this piece is still burning, light the loose ends of the kindling paper. Close the screen, and your fire is started.

A Fire Needs Air:

Burning fuel in a fireplace requires a constant supply of air. Tight weatherstripping and storm sashes may not permit enough air to enter the house to sustain the fire properly. Chances are you have installed ventilating brick as recommended on Pages 71 and 72. If more air is needed, open a window a few inches. Sometimes leaving the door to the basement open will do the job.

Watch out for the effect of ventilating fans. Even a small kitchen fan exhausts a surprising amount of air from the house. If there is no way to replace this air, except down the chimney, your fireplace will smoke and, in extreme cases, ashes may be drawn out onto the hearth extension, even through the closed screen.

Putting it out — Safely:

If your fire hasn't burned itself out by bedtime, use a pair of fire tongs to stand any unburned logs on end in the back corners of the fireplace. In this position they will soon burn out, and you will have some good kindling ready for the next fire. Do not close the damper while smoldering or burning fuel remains! Be sure the screen is closed to keep random sparks and embers off the floor or rugs.

Some Do's and Don'ts:

Don't be disappointed or impatient if the fire seems to die out in its early stages. A first-of-the-season fire may need more kindling or perhaps another half-sheet of newspaper burned to warm the flue.

Most important — let a bed of ashes accumulate under the fuel. Not too thick — about an inch or so deep — but spread around evenly over the whole hearth area. The ashes insulate the cold hearth and your later fires will start much more readily.

Don't try to build too big a fire. Three logs are ideal and four should be all you will ever need for a comfortable, cozy evening. As the top and front logs burn up, turn them with the tongs, placing a fresh log on top.

Keep your fireplace screen closed, especially when leaving the room as sparks might pop out unobserved to smolder on floor or rug. Always remember to OPEN the damper when starting a fire — CLOSE damper when the fire is completely out.

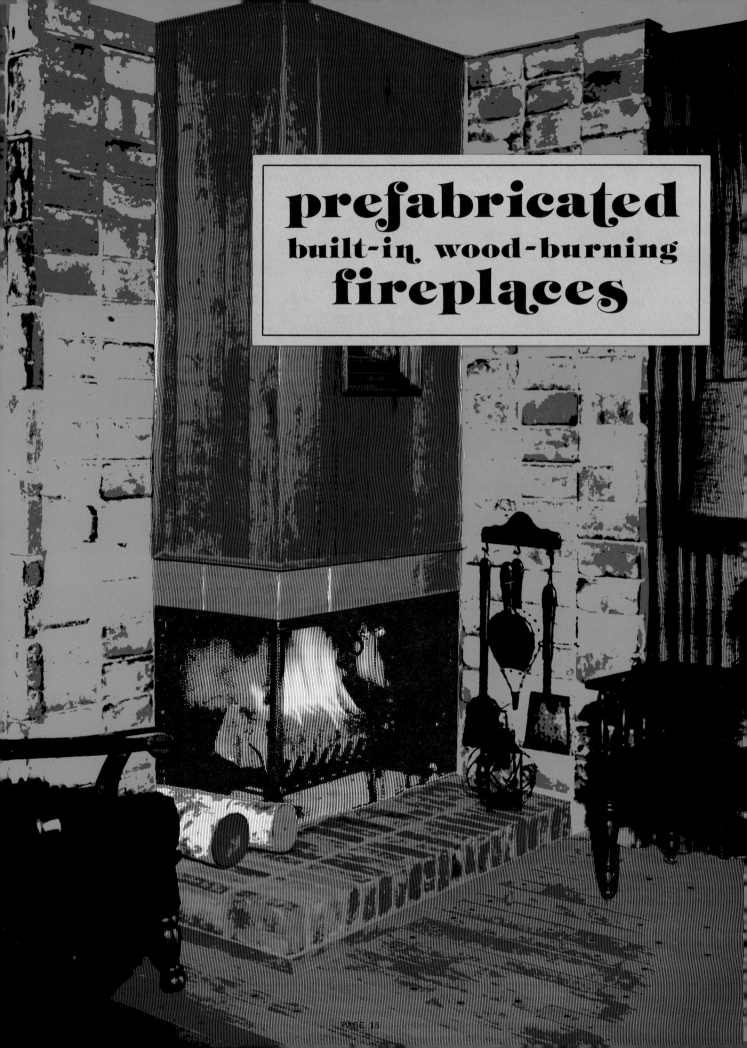

prefabricated
built-in, wood-burning
fireplaces

Majestic Thulman® wood-burning fireplaces

Prefabricated fireplaces are uniquely engineered to be the most modern and economical method of building a fireplace into the home today. With the advent of the factory-built unit, it is becoming the conventional way to install a fireplace that anyone can afford.

This section shows just a few of the innumerable ways for installing and finishing Majestic Built-In fireplaces to add warmth, comfort and design compatibility without construction limitations or the high cost of full-masonry construction. The fireplace-and-chimney units are designed for easy installation, with ordinary tools, in any type of construction — upstairs, downstairs, or on each floor, stacked one above the other.

Majestic Built-In fireplaces are compact, ready-to-install fireplaces — front-opening and corner models — complete with built-in damper, divided fire screen, and pre-finished one piece surround. Each unit has the firebrick in place and is prepared for installation of a gas starter. Unitized and pre-built, the complete system installs adjacent to wood beams, joists or wall materials and sets on existing floor. Builds into or on any wall in any location; and shelves, closets or cabinets may be built beside the fireplace to give complete latitude for individual design and finish styling.

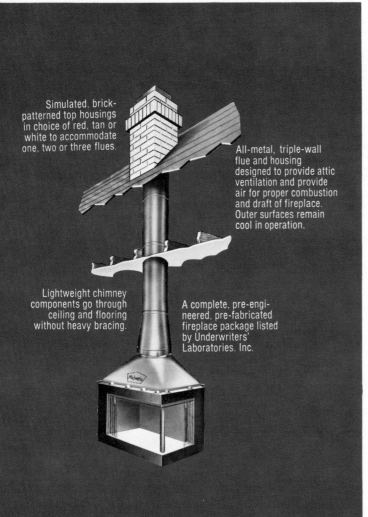

Simulated, brick-patterned top housings in choice of red, tan or white to accommodate one, two or three flues.

All-metal, triple-wall flue and housing designed to provide attic ventilation and provide air for proper combustion and draft of fireplace. Outer surfaces remain cool in operation.

Lightweight chimney components go through ceiling and flooring without heavy bracing.

A complete, pre-engineered, pre-fabricated fireplace package listed by Underwriters' Laboratories, Inc.

Thermo-Siphoning Principle

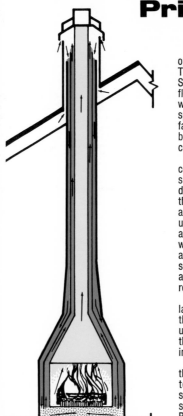

Dependable wood-burning fireplace operation is no gamble with Majestic Thulman fireplaces. The Thermo-Siphoning principle is a patented air flow system that utilizes a triple-walled chimney of three positive spaced concentric pipes to a special factory-built chimney top. The firebox is insulated by air chambers that coincide with those in the flue pipe.

The illustration clearly shows how cool air (green area) enters the outside cooling duct and is circulated down and around the firebox and up through the middle chamber (red area). This thermo-siphoning allows using the air as insulation while hot air is expelled at the chimney top with products of combustion (yellow area). Baffles in the chimney top separate the flue outlet from the cool air inlet so waste gases are not recirculated.

This system gives excellent insulation, proper draft and control of the burning process. The smoke goes up the chimney and the warmth of the burning fire delightfully radiates into the room.

The firebox floor and walls have thick ceramic lining. The entire system can be easily supported on standard wood flooring in complete safety. (Example: a 36" Majestic Built-In, wood burning fireplace and components for a modern one-story house weigh less than 400 pounds.)

There was a time when no builder or home owner would think of framing-in a fireplace with anything but brick, stone, concrete block or other masonry or non-combustible materials.

However, the recent introduction of the all-metal, factory-built fireplace has changed the basic requirements of fireplace construction. With this pre-engineered and pre-proportioned unit, it is now possible — and quite advantageous — to build in a genuine, wood-burning fireplace *without using a single brick, stone, concrete block or ounce of mortar!*

On the pages immediately following are a number of room scenes, showing a few of the ways in which pre-built fireplaces may be finished and trimmed. You will notice that, although brick and other masonry materials are *not needed* for these installations, they may be used in a veneer finish if desired.

Remodelers have taken to the pre-built fireplace as a relatively easy and economical way to enhance the appearance and value of older homes.

Times Have Changed!

Modern house and fireplace construction, completely pre-built from hearth to chimney top, is a far cry from Early American times when the "quaint" old fireplace formed the nucleus of the home.

In 1745, Benjamin Franklin wrote this about early fireplaces: "They almost always smoke if the door be not left open. They require a large funnel, and a large funnel carries off a great quantity of air, which occasions what is called a strong draft to the chimney without which strong draft the smoke would come out of some part or other of so large an opening, so that the door can seldom be shut; and the cold air so nips the back and heels of those that sit before the fire, that they have no comfort till either screens or settles are provided (at considerable expense) to keep it off which both cumber the room, and darken the fireside."

Complete works of Benjamin Franklin, edited by Jared Sparks, Boston, 1838, Vol. VI, pp. 324-325.

Majestic® Thulman® Fireplaces

All Majestic Thulman units are shipped with matte black surrounds for finished installations if desired. The angled casings permit space-saving corner installations and are prepared for easy installation of gas log lighter. A hardened collar at top of units always assures a round starter for easy attachment of flue sections. The strong metal firebox is lined with heat-resistant material and further insulated by a unique three casing design to provide inner air spaces to keep outer surfaces cool by utilizing air drawn only from outside. The basic unit has zero clearance to combustibles and eliminates the need for masonry or heavy footings. The pre-pleated black mesh fire screen, with attractive brass pulls, is factory installed and wrapped for protection.

All specific fireplace-chimney package components are determined by individual installation requirements and supplied to specifications. Write for detailed ordering and installation instructions.

28″

The smallest of the Majestic factory-built fireplaces has a full 28″ wide by 22″ high opening. Available only in a front-open model. The tapered firebox and compact size make this model ideal for space saving corner installations. From inside corner of room to face of unit requires only 37″ of normally wasted space. Approximately 8.6 square feet of floor area when the installation is enclosed.

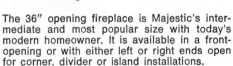

36″

The 36″ opening fireplace is Majestic's intermediate and most popular size with today's modern homeowner. It is available in a front-opening or with either left or right ends open for corner, divider or island installations.

42″

The commanding size of these 42″ opening units creates a dominating fireside center of attraction. Available with either right or left side open. The firescreen on all models opens from front center and encloses entire firebox opening.

Stacking

Majestic Thulman Fireplaces are designed to permit multi-floor stacking installations with all units on center. By the proper selection of Majestic 3-wall air insulated chimney components, multiple fireplaces, or a combination with other appliances, may be vented in a common top termination. A multiple or unusual installation plan book is available from The Majestic Company with most problems previously solved and diagramed.

any location—any room any type of home

One of the main reasons the prefabricated fireplace is gaining so much prominence as the conventional method of building a fireplace is the lack of restrictions on placement. In fact, almost any installation is possible with a Majestic Thulman fireplace and Majestic components. However, from the standpoint of economics, it is well to keep two basic thoughts in mind.

First, select a location so that joists, trusses and rafters will not have to be cut when installing the chimney. Second, select a location so that, when installed, the chimney top extends at least two or more feet above the roof peak when within 10' of the peak. When further than 10' from the peak, the top of the chimney should be positioned so that it is 10' or more from the closest point on the roof in a horizontal direction, and 2' above that point. (Applies also to any draft obstructions such as trees or other buildings.)

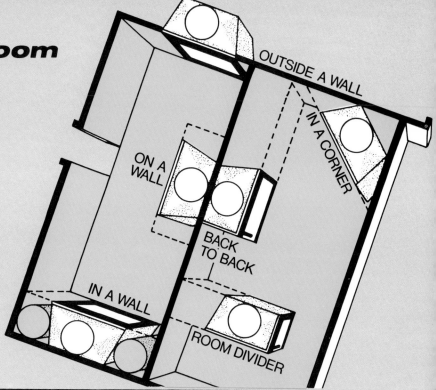

STRAIGHT UP INSTALLATION

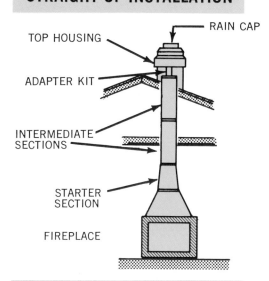

ELBOW INSTALLATION

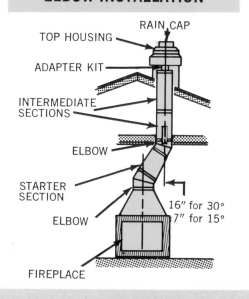

16" for 30°
7" for 15°

Prefabricated fireplaces have flexibility of installations

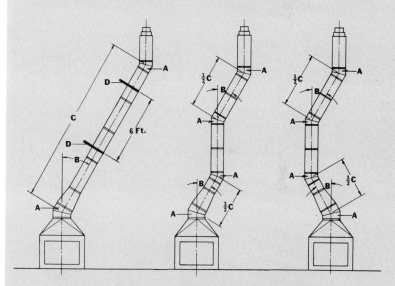

TYPICAL DOUBLE OFFSET INSTALLATIONS

RESTRICTIONS:
A. Four 30° elbows maximum per system.

B. Chimney is to be a maximum of 30° from vertical.

C. Maximum of 20 ft. total length of angled run of chimney.

D. Additional support to be provided every 6 ft. from angled run of chimney.

Keep in mind, when choosing the location for your fireplace, the straight up installation is always the economical method. But elbow and double offset installations, even though more components are used, make a fireplace a reality in locations where masonry installations would either not be possible or prohibitive in cost.

Majestic Thulman Chimneys - Gas Vents - Components

Majestic TOP HOUSINGS and FLUE TERMINATIONS for any style of installation

TRADITIONAL tops have simulated brick patterns in a choice of red, tan or white. Single, double, triple or extra tall single flue types available. Matching extensions 36″ high are also available. Simulated flue tile caps are available blank, open with 3-baffles or with flat, rain-proof hood.

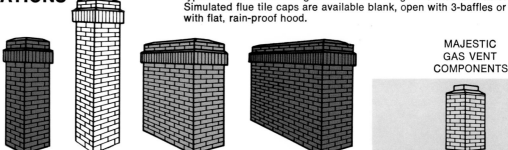

T18   **TL18**   **T40**   **T62**

MAJESTIC GAS VENT COMPONENTS

TYPE E TOP HOUSINGS
Realistic brick pattern, red, tan or white. Includes rain cap, flashing, and adjustable telescoping pipe (5″ through 8″ diameter).

WINDCAP-ROUND TOP
Attractive, low styled silhouette to terminate a vent where no top housing is desired. Tested under extreme wind conditions.

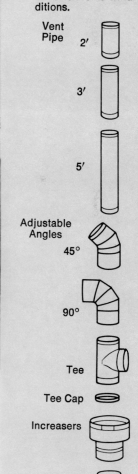

Vent Pipe   2′

3′

5′

Adjustable Angles

45°

90°

Tee

Tee Cap

Increasers

Adjustable vent length

Flashing   Collar

MAJESTIC CHIMNEY COMPONENTS

 1′ sections

 1½′

 2′

 3′

 Flashing

 Firestop for multi-levels

 Studio base for cathedral ceilings (Contemporary fireplaces)

 Ceiling, support starter base for all purpose chimney

 15° Elbows

 30° Elbows

 Support

 Starter used with Majestic Thulman Fireplaces

CONTEMPORARY round or square tops may be used to top a free-standing stack for a slender silhouette or for chimneys terminating at the top of a chase with flat roof.

TC   **TSL**

TCL

When special or unusual chimney effects are desired for architectural design or motif, chases may be built using Majestic round or square top housings and certain clearances and ventilation, described in a separate bulletin available from your dealer.

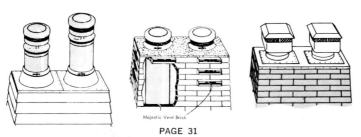

Majestic Vent Brick

Set fireplace in any location and enclose with 2 x 4 framing. (No footers or special supports needed.)

Triple-wall flue sections may elbow and return in minimum space to clear obstructions.

Conceal flue and framing with any type wall material. (U. L. listed for zero clearance to combustibles).

Cut roof opening — install flashing and add chimney sections through opening.

Terminate with top housing of your choice. See page 31 for options available.

Prefabricated, T-18 simulated brick top housing with flat rain cap shown installed.

An unusual installation—fast and simple with Majestic® Thulman®

Throughout this book, we show attractive fireplaces in individual room settings. Many homes not only have fireplaces in the living room and family room, but also have a hearth in the master bedroom, den or family kitchen. Multiple fireplace installations can be carefully planned to utilize one chimney housing for several fireplaces. It is both practical and economical to install factory-built fireplaces (as shown on pages 15 to 40) in existing rooms that, when finished, will blend in with the original decor.

prefabricated built-in gas-fired fireplaces

The Majestic Gasilator series offers you fireplace charm, maximum operating convenience and safety with easiest possible installation in three popular sizes. The realistic log set in oak design displays a distinctive flame pattern that gives wood fire realism without the chore of toting logs and removing ashes. These natural gas units are provided with an automatic and combination control valve and pressure regulator with 100% safety shut-off feature — easily converted to liquid petroleum.

To light the Majestic Gasilator, you merely flick the lever control located on center front of the hearth and it automatically opens the damper before the main burner ignites. This unique feature, working through an interlocking control and self-generating power pile, needs no outside electric or house current and is absolutely foolproof. When fireplace is not operating, the damper is always closed, thereby eliminating drafts or outside air coming through the unit.

gas-fired Fireplaces...
ith interlocking control switch

28"
Gasilator®
FULL 28" x 22" SCREENED OPENING

36"
Gasilator®
FULL 36" x 24" SCREENED OPENING

42"
Gasilator®
FULL 42" x 27" SCREENED OPENING

● Design certified by American Gas Association to ANSI standards. ● 0" clearance to rear, sides and floor. ● Gas supply plumbed through floor, side or back to factory-installed control valve. ● Wiring and gas connections conveniently accessible through removable hearth plate with unit installed. ● Hearth level control for air-mixture adjustment. ● Integral cast-iron grate bar gives attractive log basket appearance.

The basic units are shipped assembled, screens in place, ready to install with a one-piece black surround ideally suited for finished installation — or Gasilator can be trimmed with your choice of any material for exterior design. With a 2" non-combustible trim above fireplace opening, the entire Gasilator has "zero" clearance with minimum unit depth to allow space-saving in-the-wall installation using all types of building materials abutting unit. Gasilators are engineered and designed to connect to any approved existing flue or standard type B gas vent. Elbows may be used at any height. See gas vent components, page 31.

All Majestic compact Gasilators have been designed, engineered and tested to comply with leading building codes and meet the high standards typical of fireplaces from Majestic.

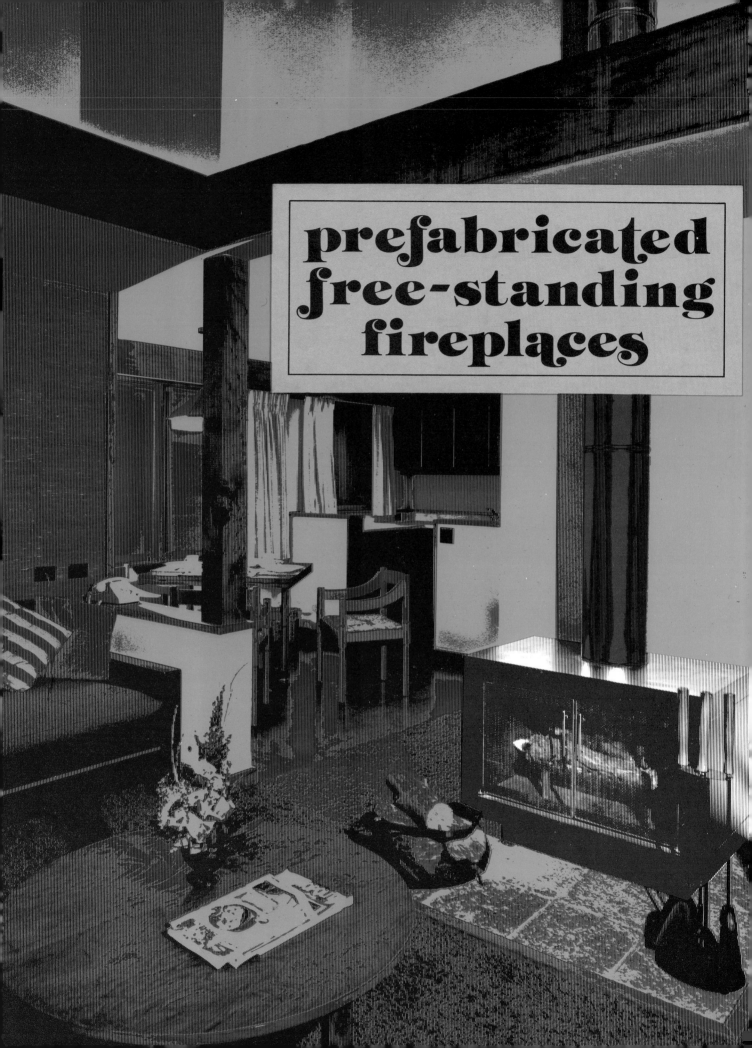

prefabricated
free-standing
fireplaces

Majestic Contemporary Fireplaces

imaginative fireplace charm
....a new era of self-expression

Crackling open fire has traditionally symbolized hospitality in the home. A good place to be together . . . where the hearth charms in imaginative ways.

For the individualistic taste of the modern, creative homemaker, Majestic Contemporary Fireplaces—the work of up-to-the-minute designers — add new zest and individually stylize the home of today.

STYLES . . . various shapes, sizes and designs to highlight the full range of room motifs and permit installation most anywhere.

COLORS . . . expressive shades reflecting vitality for living are decorator coordinated. Color swatches at right approximate either porcelain or enamel colors as are available for each model. Aztec colors are stippled with black.

FUELS . . . authentic Wood-Burning or convenient, efficient Gas-Fired and Electric units assure a fireplace for everyone.

INSTALLATION . . . easy to install from hearth to chimney top with Majestic components. See Pages 31 and 52.

Let your imagination run free . . . choose a Majestic Contemporary Fireplace to satisfy that irresistable urge toward self-expression in your home, apartment or leisure home.

SELECT

From the pictures and descriptions given in this chapter, you can easily choose the free-standing, wall-hanging or suspended fireplace that is just the right size, shape and color for your installation. Each fireplace requiring a flue is packed with enough pipe for an 8' ceiling. The universal adapter included allows for normal height variances and different thicknesses of protective floor coverings required for all combustible floors.

Available colors shown are: 1–Matte Black, 2–Mandarin Red, 3–White, 4–Inca Gold, 5–Bronze Green, 6–Orange Tone

IF PRODUCT OR PERFORMANCE DEFECTIVE
★
Good Housekeeping
GUARANTEES
REPLACEMENT OR REFUND TO CONSUMER

THIS GUARANTY APPLIES ONLY TO
Majestic COMPONENTS...
NOT INSTALLATION

Majestic firehood®

the original conical Wood-Burning Fireplace

Accepted as the trend setter, the Firehood is today's most popular free-standing fireplace. Coordinated geometric shapes in five sparkling porcelain colors or the popular matte black result in a dramatic and functional unit. The conical hood and slender stack combine readily with formal, rustic, provincial or modern decor in a new or existing home. Hearth and firebox opening are designed to permit full view of a crackling fire from most any room position. Two hearth sizes, 38″ and 45″, assure a Firehood proportioned for any room. The 45″ Firehood is available in matte black only. Included with pre-assembled unit are free-standing folding screen, universal adapter, ready-mix refractory hearth material and enough matching pipe for an 8′ ceiling. Log basket grate is optional equipment.

aztec®
a dramatic concept in a Wood-Burning Fireplace

The Aztec represents a new era in fireplace design. This totally different and universally unique creation provides a dramatic effect in any room location. All matte black or black stippled colorful porcelain finished fire chamber, accentuated by a matte black spun steel base and vertical flue, offers truly unusual beauty. One piece, removable screen permits ready access to firebox in either 32″ or 36″ diameter version. Double-wall construction requires no refractory hearth and permits minimum clearance to combustible walls. Screen, universal adapter and matte black pipe for an 8′ ceiling included with unit. Log basket grate is optional equipment.

manchester - piece®
a new dimension in fireplaces

Crisp, clean, straight-line rectangular styling of the Manchester-Pierce creates geometrical dimension to a modern room setting . . . and as versatile for room arrangements as a piece of modern furniture.

It may be located anyplace in a room as a free-standing unit with exposed vertical stack; for a dramatic effect use the optional rear flue model. Both models have double insulated wall construction with steel hearth and full 28″ x 16″ screened opening. Where there is no existing flue in which to tap the Manchester-Pierce, the Majestic® Thulman® all-purpose chimney shown on Pages 31 and 52 can be utilized to economically complete the installation. Included with both pre-assembled fireplace models, as standard equipment, are hinged screens and built-in damper. Available in popular matte black finish only. Top vent model includes universal adapter and matte black pipe to install to an 8′ ceiling. Log basket grate is optional but necessary equipment.

The Majestic Regency, featuring the exclusive "Silent Butler" ash drawer is eye-appealing and easy-to-install. This 24″ x 36″ wood burner is distinctively tapered to the slender 8″ round flue, colorfully finished with any of the porcelain colors or matte black. Hinged fire screens, basket grate and firebrick are installed at factory. Unit shipped with enough matching pipe to accommodate an 8′ ceiling installation.

The patented "Silent Butler" ash drawer collects ashes through a built-in ash dump for clean, tidy removal. The drawer automatically closes when removed and opens to receive ashes when replaced.

U.S. Patent No. 3421495

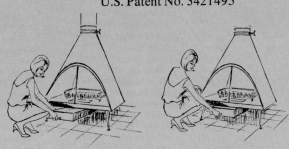

regency free-standing

Your choice of an enclosed base or tripod legs adds to the variety of either wood or gas-fired Regency installation appearances.

Where wood is not readily available or cannot be used, the gas-fired Regency offers an amazingly realistic log hearth-fire with cleanliness and convenience. The enameled or matte black units are trimmed with brass accents and shipped pre-assembled with screens, logs, natural gas burner and pressure regulator. Base unit also includes matching pipe for an 8′ ceiling. See choice of colors available on Page 43.

gas

tudor ™

A floor-to-ceiling self-contained, wood-burning fireplace that combines the time-proven Majestic® Thulman® thermo-siphoning principle in a free-standing/wall-hanging unit that requires no extensive remodeling for hearth-side enjoyment. The full 32″ screened opening lets the dancing firelight gaily reflect on the integral stainless steel hearth. The graceful sweep of either the embossed steel pewter or matte black hood, trimmed with stainless steel, adapts to ceiling heights of 6′10″ to 8′0″. The Tudor is uniquely insulated to simply set on any combustible floor and against existing wall material. Easy installation is completed with Majestic triple-wall chimney and roof termination of your choice as shown on Pages 31 and 52. The black Tudor may be painted with wall paint to match or contrast at redecorating time if desired. Underwriters' Laboratories, Inc. listed.

wall-hanging

doric ™

Push-button, open-fire charm with picture-hanging installation ease describes the new compact Doric. Finished in decorator-inspired, patterned steel in the preferred choice of enamel colors, this distinctive unit is highlighted with dual black mantels. Also finished in black, a ceiling-high flue wrapper conceals the gas vent whether it be elbowed through the wall or straight up through the ceiling.

A switch located on the hearth center front automatically activates natural looking gas logs. Like magic, double logs complete with grate bars appear to be afire, producing a realistic, varicolored flame. No house current is required to hook up either the natural or L.P. gas units. Both units are easily connected and serviced.

Imaginative decorators can include a 34¼″x39″x15½″ Doric in the room decor with no sacrifice of floor space. The Doric, too, may be trimmed with accenting ornaments to complement room motif.

mercury™
enjoyable from any angle

Designed for viewing the wood-burning fire a full 360°, the Mercury is available in either 36″ or 42″ diameters. The basic unit consists of either colored porcelain (36″ model only) or matte black hood, with black pipe to an 8′ ceiling, circle screen, hearth pan and ready-mix refractory material. By selecting the optional chain set for hanging installation, or pedestal for free-standing unit, a modern flair with masculine ruggedness is achieved in any residential or commercial installation. The basic unit also may be nested in a custom masonry firebox, as shown below, to create a dramatic conversation pit.

venus®
locates close to wall

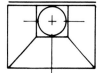

The durable all-steel construction of the Venus assures fulfillment of that nostalgic desire for an open hearth fire without involving wall construction. Built-in construction features allow minimum back and side wall clearance to conserve valuable floor space. Matte black pipe and brass trim complement any of the porcelain colors or matte black finish. Accent trim of your personal choice may be used to decorate the uninterrupted front panel.

Included with the 36″ wide, pre-assembled Venus are sliding screen, damper, refractory hearth material and enough matte black pipe for ceilings in the range of 7′ 9¾″ to 8′ 9¼″. Log basket grate is optional equipment.

VENUS TOP VIEW

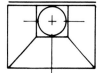

ATHENA TOP VIEW

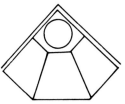

athena®
goes in a corner

A companion design to the Venus, with the added functional feature of 90° design for compact installation in a corner. Convert what is often wasted space into a stunning focal point and make any room a more enjoyable place to be together.

jupiter®
a decorator's delight

These wood-burning fire-cones are available in three sizes to fit any room or budget. The 24″ and 30″ models feature free formed hoods in a choice of porcelain colors or matte black with black circular bases. Overall heights are 44″ and 56″. The 38″ model has a commanding 77″ height and distinctive converging line effect tooled into the angled curved hood; and is available in matte black only. All models include clam-shell type firescreens, supported on tracks with roller bearings to assure easy access to the hearth, and matching pipe to an 8′ ceiling. Grates are optional equipment available from your Majestic dealer.

TYPICAL INSTALLATIONS USING
MAJESTIC® THULMAN® CHIMNEYS

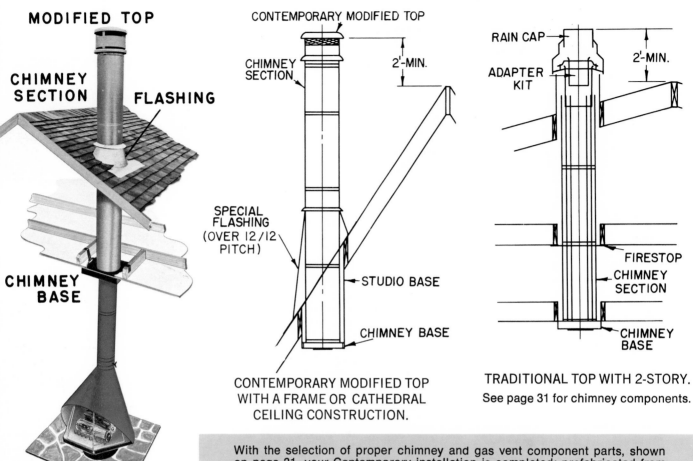

MODIFIED TOP

CHIMNEY SECTION

FLASHING

CHIMNEY BASE

CONTEMPORARY

CONTEMPORARY MODIFIED TOP

CHIMNEY SECTION

2'-MIN.

SPECIAL FLASHING (OVER 12/12 PITCH)

STUDIO BASE

CHIMNEY BASE

CONTEMPORARY MODIFIED TOP WITH A FRAME OR CATHEDRAL CEILING CONSTRUCTION.

RAIN CAP

ADAPTER KIT

2'-MIN.

FIRESTOP

CHIMNEY SECTION

CHIMNEY BASE

TRADITIONAL TOP WITH 2-STORY.
See page 31 for chimney components.

With the selection of proper chimney and gas vent component parts, shown on page 31, your Contemporary installation is completed; prefabricated from hearth to chimney top, without construction limitations or excessive labor. To vent into an existing flue, consult your applicable local code requirements before starting. All Majestic fireplaces, chimneys and gas vents are approved, listed, certified and/or accepted by leading national and local building codes and authorities.

electric fireplaces

hospitality series
.....heater optional

Majestic Electric Fireplaces install in minutes—easy as a picture to hang. Place on any wall of any room, plug into an electric outlet, and "like magic" the decorative fireplace, complete with sliding screens and realistic "flame-flickering" electric logs, produces instant hospitality. Make any of the three Hospitality designs a heat source by adding a heating unit. Thermostatically controlled forced air heat, up to 13,600 BTU, adds utility to each model in the Hospitality series. Two optional heater packages are available that conceal in the base of each unit and operate either from a 120 volt outlet or a permanently wired 240 volt circuit.

The Monticello® is an elegant Colonial style in matte black with scalloped brass trim around the hood. For extra decoration and "Early American" flair, a cast antiqued bronze eagle is available.

The Cortez® has a white leatherette covered steel hood to contrast with the black ornamental grille work on each side for a Spanish flavor.

The Caprice® features wood grained side panels and mantel with reversible leatherette covered front panel—hunter red on one side and white on reverse side—customized with owner's initial.

space-saver series...... heater built-in

APOLLO® 4
Entire unit finished in
rich matte black.

APOLLO® 5
Base finished in matte black
with red satin hood.

Where space is at a premium and the decorative charm of a fireplace is wanted, the Space-Saver Series is the answer. Apollo® models feature all-metal, contemporary design which blends with a wide variety of motifs and yet are economical. Removable firescreen adds realism to the flickering log set. The hearth of the fireplace contains a forced air, thermostatically controlled 1650 watt heater which yields 5640 BTU. Plugging into a 120 volt outlet, the log set and heater are controlled by conveniently located finger tip control switch.

Majestic Space-Saver Fireplaces are ideal for small homes, mobile homes, and apartments, and are also supplemental heaters . . . requiring only 30″ x 50″ of wall space—12½″ deep.

Install a fireplace as easily as hanging a picture. Easy to take down when moving — or changing fireplace to another room.

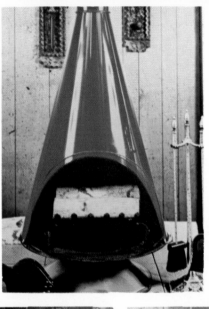
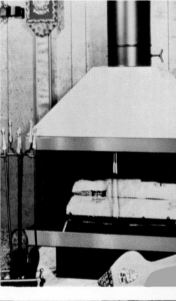

conventional masonry fireplaces

proper construction of masonry fireplaces

The most attractively finished fireplace is just a cold, empty space unless it comes alive frequently with dancing flames and gleaming embers. And a masonry fireplace will not do this unless it is correctly proportioned, sealed, vented and "laid up" from start to finish.

As an extension of our earlier chapter on the definition of a fireplace, let us consider more specifically the size of the separate parts and how they must relate to one another when considering a full masonry fireplace. The following diagrams and notes will describe the important size ratios.

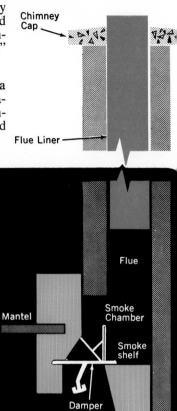

Chimney Cap

Flue Liner

Flue

Smoke Chamber

Smoke shelf

Mantel

Damper

Firebox

Ash dump

Hearth

Ash Pit

Ash Pit Door

Basement Floor

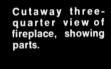

Cutaway three-quarter view of fireplace, showing parts.

NOTE: Experts differ over the exact proportions to be used in fireplace construction. The figures given in this book are approximate, since circumstances of individual fireplace installations are seldom identical.

Section* view of fireplace, showing parts.

*Throughout this book, references are made to "plan" (top), "elevation" (front), and "section" (side) view.

How Big?

Size of fireplace versus room size is an important relationship. A firebox opening 30 to 36 inches wide is suitable for any room with approximately 300 square feet of floor space. Another useful rule is: 5 square inches of fireplace opening to each square foot of floor area in small rooms, reducing the proportion in larger rooms.

In deciding on size, keep in mind that the fires built in the fireplace should match its capacity. Too small a fire in a large firebox lacks heating efficiency. On the other hand, the fireplace with a burning fire should never resemble the inside of a blast furnace.

In planning the shape of your fireplace opening, remember that the height of the opening should be about 2/3 to 3/4 the width.

What Materials?

Common brick is a popular fireplace material, though concrete block or natural stone may also be used for the main construction. Firebrick or other refractory material must be used to line the firebox, and firebrick or flue tile should also comprise the inner course of the flue. Firebrick or flue tile should be laid in fireclay, with outer walls laid in regular masonry mortar. All joints should be tightly sealed to prevent smoke leakage and to assure steady, sufficient draft. Of course, any non-combustible material may be used to surround the firebox opening and as a surface on the exterior hearth. Any combustible material may be used as trim, so long as safe clearance distances are observed (at least 6" from firebox opening).

Where to Build It

Where you build your fireplace in your house will depend on convenience, available draft, appearance, and how you wish your chimney to look in relation to the exterior of your house (since the chimney must rise at least two feet higher than the highest roof peak).

Whether the fireplace is located on one side, or at the end, of a rectangular-shaped room is up to the individual's taste. Corner fireplaces, in L-shaped rooms or as room dividers, are increasingly popular and are discussed in the Multi-Opening chapter, Page 79 and the Prefabricated Fireplace chapter, Page 15.

Structural support is a paramount consideration, since great weight is involved in a full masonry fireplace. The fireplace and chimney must rest on a firm concrete footing. The design of your home, the "lay of the land" and the soil condition may limit your choice of location.

Costs can be cut on the installation of two fireplaces in a single home if they are laid up back-to-back or one above the other as in first floor and basement rooms. The flues are thus built into the same chimney. A fireplace with openings in two adjoining rooms is also an interesting possibility. (See Multi-Opening Fireplaces—Page 79.)

The Foundation

A definite ratio of foundation size to fireplace and chimney weight has been determined to prevent cracking and/or settling. A solid concrete foundation (or footing) 36" deep and 6" wider and longer than the chimney plan, is usually sufficient. Consult your local building code, since these codes differ according to existing soil and moisture conditions in individual areas. If total weight is needed to determine the depth of the foundation required, figure brick at 130 pounds (and concrete at 150 pounds) per cubic foot. For cubic footage, figure entire cross section volume, including the open portion of the flue.

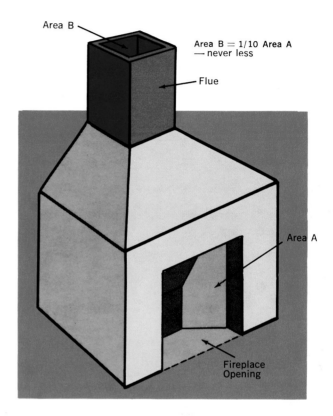

Area B

Area B = 1/10 Area A
— never less

Flue

Area A

Fireplace Opening

Firebox and Flue Opening

The cross section area of the flue opening (area B in above sketch) must be at least 1/10 that of the firebox opening facing the room (Area A) for chimneys 15 ft. high or over, and 1/8 for chimneys under 15 ft. This proportion has been worked out through many years of fireplace building experience at Majestic and elsewhere. Less than these areas will produce a smoky, choked-off, poorly drafted fireplace. Much more will give you an unnecessarily broad flue, perhaps an excess of downdraft, and an entrance for unwanted rainwater. The elevation, plan and section drawings (Pages 60 and 62) will aid greatly in proportioning firebox and flue openings.

Draft is Vital

The lifeblood of a fire is oxygen, and it can reach your fireplace only through the air already in, or entering, your home. In the modern, nearly air-tight, home construction, provisions for a fresh air inlet are often overlooked. (In the old days, there were chinks galore to let in air.) Opening a window slightly will often cure a smoky fireplace. Better yet, if the home is too air-tight, install ventilating brick (such as the Majestic Model 428 described on Page 72) or other ventilating device in the fireplace foundation, or basement wall or window. Study the diagrams, charts and drawings on these pages for rules in proportioning openings.

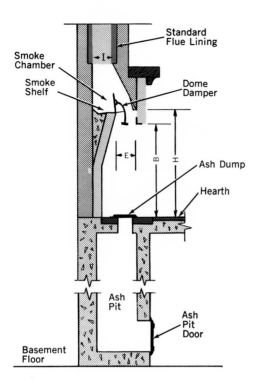

The table at the right shows all essential dimensions needed for successful fireplace construction. (See Pages 70, 71, 72 and 84 for descriptions of Majestic dampers and other components.)

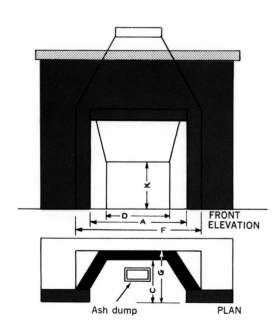

Chimney Construction

Walls — All walls of exterior and interior chimneys without linings, and exposed walls of exterior chimneys, must be at least 8″ thick when made of brick. The walls of an interior chimney with flue linings must be at least 4″ thick, and all interior chimneys should have 8″ thick walls from below the roof to the chimney top. Where two or more flues are built into a single chimney, they should be separated by one brick division or "wythe" of 4″ (or a double flue tile may be used). The walls of stone chimneys should be at least 12″ thick.

Flue — The flue must be a strong, vertical channel with reasonably smooth inside surfaces to carry off smoke rapidly. The lining must be able to withstand rapid, frequent temperature changes and should be made of fireclay not less than ⅝″ thick. Standard flue tile is suitable. All joints should be thoroughly sealed with a rich mortar. When flue tile is omitted, an 8″ thick masonry liner (preferably firebrick) should be used.

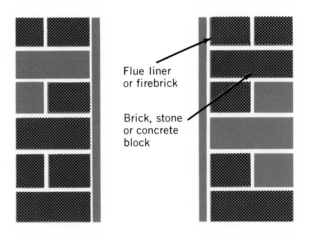

Flue liner or firebrick

Brick, stone or concrete block

Finished Opening						Dimensions				
A	B	C	D	E	F	Rough Masonry G	H	I	K	
Width	Height	Depth	Back	Throat	Width	Depth	Smoke Shelf Height	Smoke Chamber	Vertical Back	Inside of Brick Flue	Standard Flue Lining
24	28	16	16	9	30	19	32	11	14	8½x 8½	8½x 8½
26	28	16	18	9	32	19	32	11	14	8½x 8½	8½x 8½
28	28	16	20	9	34	19	32	11	14	8 x12	8½x13
30	30	16	22	9	36	19	34	11	15	8 x12	8½x13
32	30	16	24	9	38	19	34	11	15	8 x12	8½x13
34	30	16	26	9	40	19	34	11	15	12 x12	8½x13
36	31	18	27	9	42	21	36	11	16	12 x12	13 x13
38	31	18	29	9	44	21	36	11	16	12 x12	13 x13
40	31	18	31	9	46	21	36	11	16	12 x12	13 x13
42	31	18	33	9	48	21	36	11	16	12 x12	13 x13
44	32	18	35	9	50	21	37	11	17	12 x12	13 x13
46	32	18	37	9	52	21	37	11	17	12 x16	13 x13
48	32	20	38	9	54	23	37	15½	17	12 x16	13 x18
50	34	20	40	9	56	23	39	15½	18	12 x16	13 x18
52	34	20	42	9	58	23	39	15½	18	12 x16	13 x18
54	34	20	44	9	60	23	39	15½	18	16 x16	13 x18
56	36	20	46	9	62	23	41	15½	19	16 x16	18 x18
58	36	22	47	9	64	25	41	15½	19	16 x16	18 x18
60	36	22	49	9	66	25	41	15½	19	16 x16	18 x18

Capping

Draft is encouraged and chimney maintenance is reduced when a chimney cap of mortar is provided. The top surfaces of the cap should slope downward, away from the flue opening, so that moisture will drain away and protect masonry. Oncoming outside air currents will be deflected upward to promote good draft. The flue liner should project through the cap and extend above it.

When a hood is built on the chimney top, the area of the hood opening should be at least equal to the area of the flue. Concrete and brick caps are made 4″ thick and are usually projected outward 1″ or 2″ to form a drip ledge.

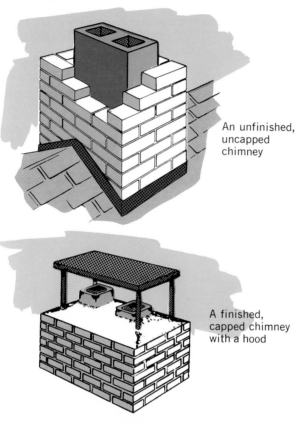

An unfinished, uncapped chimney

A finished, capped chimney with a hood

SOME THOUGHTS ON MORTAR

Brickwork around chimney flues and fireplaces should be laid with cement mortar; it is more resistant to the action of heat and flue gases than lime mortar.

A good mortar to use in setting flue linings and all chimney masonry, except firebrick, consists of 1 part Portland cement, 1 part hydrated lime (or slaked-lime putty), and 6 parts clean sand, measured by volume.

Firebrick should be laid with fireclay.

Flashing

Water leakage around chimneys can be prevented by proper flashing and counter-flashing of corrosion-resistant metal such as sheet copper. This is built into the roofing material and extends up onto the masonry. The counter-flashing is bonded into the mortar joints

and is lapped down over the flashing so that water runs *over* rather than *into* any seams. Seams may be closed with pitch or other bonding material. A "cricket" or "saddle" on the high side of a sloping roof will shed water around chimney.

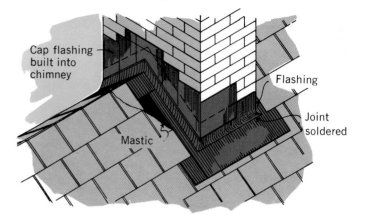

Flashing at a chimney located on a roof ridge

Cap flashing built into chimney

Flashing

Mastic

Joint soldered

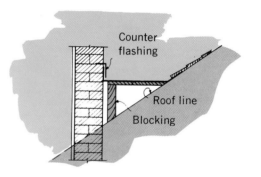

Counter flashing

Roof line

Blocking

Construction of a cricket behind a chimney

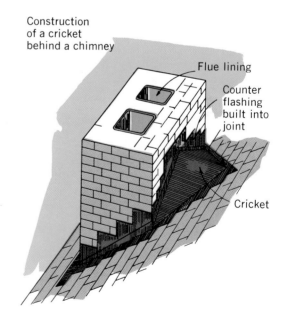

Flue lining

Counter flashing built into joint

Cricket

Insulating

The roof and all floors and walls should be framed around the chimney so that no combustible material is within 2″ of the masonry. Spaces between the framing and masonry should be filled with fireproof insulating material.

A full-masonry fireplace is the type of construction that requires the greatest amount of skill and adherence to proportioning data. To many fireplace lovers, it is the most satisfying. It requires the use of a good damper, positioned properly in the fireplace throat.

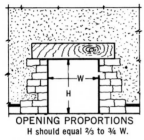

OPENING PROPORTIONS
H should equal ⅔ to ¾ W.

Start by referring to the rules, diagrams and chart on Pages 60 through 63, covering general fireplace construction. (It might be well to re-read this section, given for general fireplace background, especially if you plan to build a masonry fireplace.)

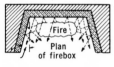

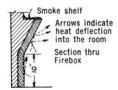

Smoke shelf

Arrows indicate heat deflection into the room

Section thru Firebox

Fire
Plan of firebox

Sides splayed 3″ for each foot of depth, or at about 15°.

The diagrams given on this page show additional basic proportions and other vital facts for a successful installation.

The least important considerations, from the standpoint of construction, are the extended hearth, mantel and surround. To be sure, they are the parts that give the fireplace a safety margin and a decorative effect; but they are not essential to operating efficiency.

Ash pit

ASH DUMP DIRECTLY BELOW FIRE

Determine the desired shape and size of your projected fireplace. The average fireplace is from 30 to 40 inches in width. The height of the fireplace and the depth from front to back do not vary to the same extent as the width. (See chart on Page 62.)

The ash dump should be placed directly below the fire on the inner hearth so the ashes may be worked through it to the ash pit below. A door to the ash pit at the level of the basement floor will make it easy to remove the ashes.

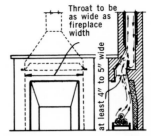

Throat to be as wide as fireplace width

at least 4″ to 5″ wide

IMPORTANCE OF THROAT DESIGN

The throat of the fireplace should always be as wide as the fireplace is wide and from four to five inches in depth. By the use of a Majestic Fireplace Damper and Throat combined, this detail of construction is automatically and satisfactorily taken care of, for each damper is properly and scientifically designed.

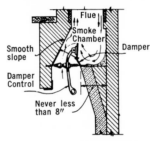

Flue
Smoke Chamber
Smooth slope
Damper
Damper Control
Never less than 8″

The back edge of the damper should always rest on the forward edge of the smoke shelf. The joint between the damper and the bottom of the smoke shelf should be tightly sealed with mortar so that it is impossible for flames to get to the flue, except through the damper throat.

A great deal of care should be used to see that proper dimensions are maintained in the smoke chamber; that the front of the wall is not drawn in so abruptly as to interfere with the rising smoke, and that all surfaces are smooth and free from large projections.

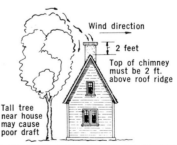

Wind direction

2 feet
Top of chimney must be 2 ft. above roof ridge

Tall tree near house may cause poor draft

CHIMNEY MUST BE HIGHER THAN CLOSE OBSTRUCTIONS

The smoke shelf should be the full width of the throat, never less than eight inches deep, and it may vary from this dimension to 12 inches or more, depending upon the depth of the fireplace itself. (See elevation sketch.)

A complete guide to dimensions and construction proportions for each size fireplace is found in the table on Page 62.

colorful! charming! imaginative!

your fireplace is what you make it ——

just a few more "idea-starters" for your wood-burning fireplace:

HF24
HF28
HF32
HF36
HF40
HF44
HF48

Back view
with damper
blade open

Formed of heavy gauge steel.
Easy-working, snug-fitting damper blade.
Handle securely fastened to strong center brace.

Series "HF" (high formed)

- Formed high, with extra wide throat for peak draft!
- No need to form throat of brick, stone or mortar!
- Built to absorb expansion and prevent cracking!

Here — for builders, masons and handymen — is more versatility of design, more ease of construction and more draft efficiency in a fireplace damper than ever before! Permits deeper downdraft shelf design without special attention to throat construction and eliminates the need for additional floor space. Made in seven lengths to meet a wide range of fireplace requirements. Strongly welded, nonbreakable heavy gauge steel construction throughout. Insulation and complete instructions are furnished with each damper.

Poker Control

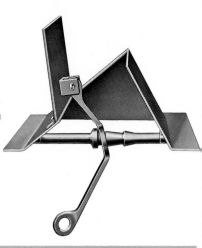

Operating ease is combined with rugged simplicity in Majestic poker-type damper controls. The operating lever has a circular opening which moves freely over the horizontal stop bar to ingeniously designed offsets for setting damper in a positive half-open, fully open or closed position.

MAJESTIC FORMED STEEL DAMPERS

Heavy gauge steel. Engineered to prevent warpage of blade and body. Flanged damper blade has poker-type control for firm seating. Specially designed for correct ratio of throat to fireplace opening to provide maximum draft and avoid smoking.

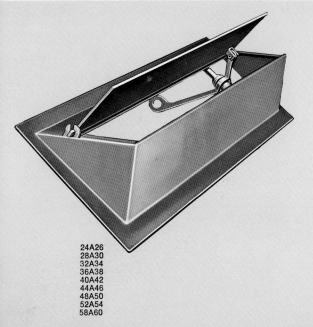

24A26
28A30
32A34
36A38
40A42
44A46
48A50
52A54
58A60

Damper No.	Width of Opening	Dimensions				Ship. Wt.
		A	B	C	D	
24A26	24″ to 26″	28¼	26¾	24	24	27
28A30	27″ to 30″	32¼	30¾	28	28	30
32A34	31″ to 34″	36¼	34¾	32	32	32
36A38	35″ to 38″	40¼	38¾	36	36	36
40A42	39″ to 42″	44¼	42¾	40	40	40
44A46	43″ to 46″	48¼	46¾	44	44	44
48A50	47″ to 50″	52¼	50¾	48	48	48
52A54	51″ to 54″	56¼	54¾	52	52	52
58A60	57″ to 60″	62½	60¾	58	58	56

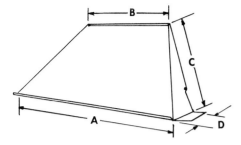

For general installation data, refer to the section and half plan drawings, and the dimensional sketch and chart, on this page. Complete instructions are fastened to each unit shipped from the factory. Additional information will be found in latest product literature for actual fireplace installation.

Half Plan

Model	Refer to Sketch of Damper				Refer to Section and Half Plan Drawings of Fireplace								
	A	B	C	D	E	F	G	H	I	J	K	L	M
HF24	24	7¼	13¾	9¾	24	26	16	16	14	10	5	8½	8½
HF28	28	11¼	13¾	9¾	28	27	16	20	14	10	5	13	8½
HF32	32	15¼	13¾	9¾	32	28	16	24	15	10	5	13	8½
HF36	36	19¼	13¾	9¾	36	29	18	27	16	10	5	13	13
HF40	40	23¼	13¾	9¾	40	30	18	31	16	10	5	13	13
HF44	44	27¼	13¾	9¾	44	31	18	35	17	10	5	13	13
HF48	48	31¼	13¾	9¾	48	32	20	38	17	10	5	18	13

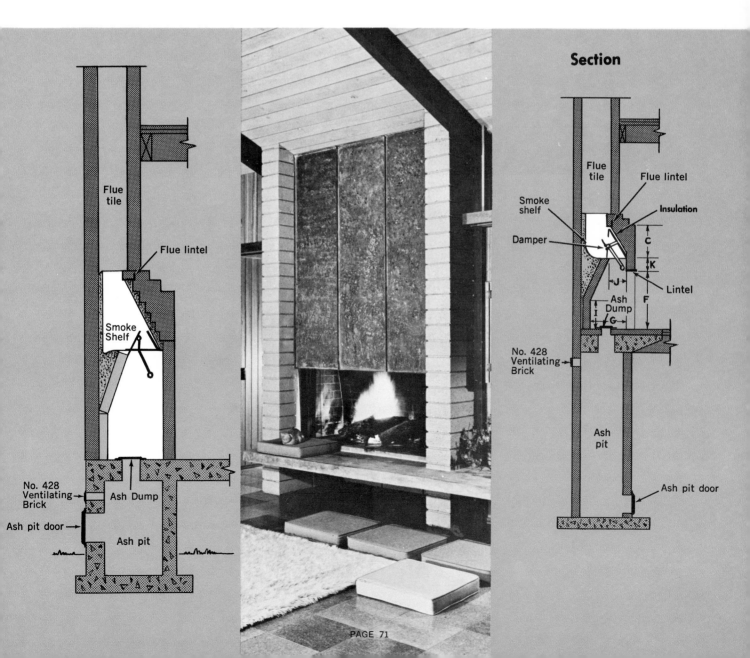

some damper installation notes—

Before starting work, make complete working drawings of the fireplace from the base to the chimney top. The basic instructions and data given in the previous chapters are helpful.

Dampers are furnished with a built-on flange for easy installation. This edge, with the damper placed far forward to assure a deep smoke shelf behind it, must rest evenly all around the top of the firebox opening and be securely mortared in position. Thus, when the damper blade is open and the fireplace is operating, an adequate smoke shelf is formed to block and deflect downdrafts and prevent smoke from pouring from the firebox opening.

Reliably made dampers close practically air tight, thus preventing loss of heat from the room when the fireplace is not in use and the damper is closed.

Dampers are designed with either poker type or rotary face controls, and some simple on-the-site assembly is usually necessary. Complete instructions for this assembly are furnished with the damper units shipped from the factory.

The advantages of the fireplace damper are sometimes overlooked: A closed damper not only prevents loss of house heat, it keeps downdrafts, wind and rain from entering the home through the chimney on chilly, inclement days. When in use, it regulates the draft, adjusting the throat opening according to the size and type of fire being burned. For example, a smoking fire may require a full throat opening while a clean log fire may need only one or two inches of opening. Closing the damper to the minimum opening (while avoiding smoking) will result in the least amount of heat loss up the chimney.

The damper affords protection against the elements — and also against wildlife. A damper carelessly left open — especially in summer — may result in an invasion by insects, squirrels or other unwanted "critters."

One of the most popular types of damper is the kind with an integral lintel. This is handiest to install.

Always remember that the full damper opening should be as big or bigger than the flue opening above it.

additional fireplace components—

Ash Dump

This 4½″ x 9″ steel or cast iron "trap door" provides a convenient outlet through which to drop ashes into an ash pit built beneath the fireplace.

Ventilating Brick

Replacing one or more standard bricks in the house foundation will admit combustion air for fireplace efficiency. The vent brick measures 4¼″ x 8″ x 2¼″ and is installed in the wall between the ash pit and the out-of-doors. (See diagrams on Page 71.)

Steel Lintels

May be used with all fireplaces of masonry. Five sizes available, 36″ to 60″ lengths. May be cut into shorter sections, if desired, to support smoke shelf or flue. All lintels are 3½″ x 3½″.

Ash Pit Doors

These doors, in cast iron or steel in five sizes, give cleanout access to the ash pit beneath the fireplace. The door is usually installed at or near the level of the basement floor or at the outside wall. 10¼″ x 10¼″ to 15¼″ x 15¼″ sizes.

Fireplace Basket Grates

The type of support most usually provided for best combustion of fireplace fuel. Steel model designed for wood is made of welded ½″ square solid bars. Six sizes available from Majestic. 13⅛″ to 17″ deep. 19¼″ to 36″ fronts. 15½″ to 32″ backs.

The warm air circulator

WHY A Majestic CIRCULATOR FIREPLACE?

Majestic's Circulator line includes six different sizes to satisfy a wide range of fireplace construction and room requirements. (See chart on Page 76.)

Smoke chamber, downdraft shelf, firebox and other components are built in. Cuts expensive, time-consuming measuring, estimating and rebuilding.

A real heat miser! Cold air intakes and warm air outlets make unit an effective circulator of warmth. Openings (with grilles) may be placed for warming one or more rooms. Grilles (and fans for forced draft) are available. (See Page 76.)

Each unit is completely pre-engineered and proportioned at the factory. Eliminates guesswork in laying up a masonry fireplace.

High, wide uniformly sloping, built-in smoke dome encourages good draft and guards against smoking to assure a correctly burning fireplace.

Lintel (ordered extra) correctly aligns top edge of opening. Eases the labor of masonry construction.

Built-in, integral damper with easy-working poker type control and tight-fitting, leak-free valve blade.

Angle seals, furnished with the unit, form a neat, tight-fitting front closing for good appearance and correct operation.

Solidly made of heavy gauge steel. Strongly welded into an efficient, versatile economical fireplace form.

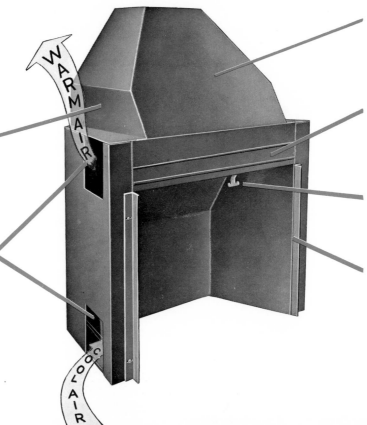

The "Circulator" idea embodies a masonry fireplace and an effective "house warmer" in one pre-engineered, pre-built metal fireplace unit.

Masonry is constructed *around* the unit, following its scientifically designed proportions. The result is a regular radiant fireplace AND a circulator fireplace that sends warm air convection currents into the room — even into adjacent rooms — through a system of strategically located intake and outlet ducts and grilles.

Specially designed blades, welded to back and sides, direct flow of air over hottest parts of unit for maximum circulation of warmth, and to increase the heat-absorbing and radiating surface area.

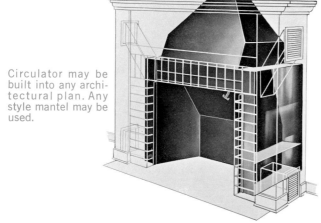

Circulator may be built into any architectural plan. Any style mantel may be used.

The Circulator is widely used by builders, masons and home handymen in installations where it is also desirable to minimize cost of masonry labor. Building in a Circulator eliminates much of the measuring, checking (and sometimes mere guesswork) involved in the construction of a conventional masonry fireplace.

Contained as integral parts of the Circulator are: firebox, damper, smoke dome, downdraft shelf, angle seals for placing masonry — even heat-boosters (such as the unique "Radiant Blades" of the Majestic Circulator fireplace).

The Circulator may be used as a between-season home heating system, on chilly days and nights when quick warmth feels good but the use of the furnace is not quite justified. Adding small fans in the warm air circulator ducts affords the added efficiency of forced-air operation.

The Majestic Company has developed the Circulator through many years of research and experience in the fireplace field.

This unit is a carefully pre-proportioned metal form around which the mason or home handyman builds the complete fireplace.

The chart on page 76 lists the sizes available, along with basic data. The data given is for typical installations. Since specifications are subject to change, it is recommended that you write to The Majestic Company, Huntington, Indiana 46750, and refer to the latest product literature for sizes of Circulators and accessories.

how to put in a Circulator —

Choose from a variety of locations, as shown in the diagrams. Complete installation instructions are shipped with each Majestic Circulator, but the following general directions will help in pre-planning.

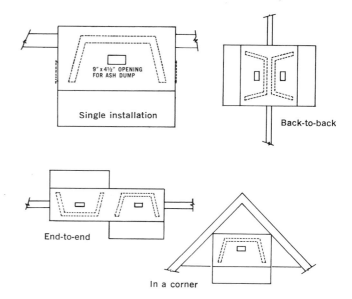

GRILLE LOCATIONS

When the Circulator sits entirely outside a wall, it is necessary for grilles to be on face of fireplace. With wall at rear, both return and warm air grilles may be placed on ends; on front; or on a combination of front and ends. Return air grilles must be at floor line, but warm air grilles (upper ones) may be opposite warm air outlet or flues built for warm air with grilles near ceiling; or masonry ducts may be constructed for discharging warm air into an adjoining room. It is imperative that masonry be built from outlets of Circulator to grilles, forming a duct for air flow.

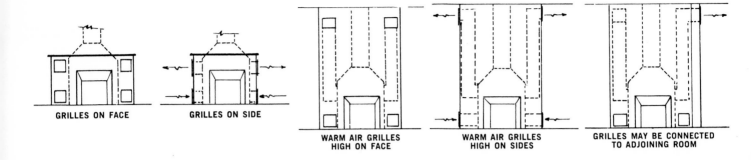

GRILLES ON FACE GRILLES ON SIDE WARM AIR GRILLES HIGH ON FACE WARM AIR GRILLES HIGH ON SIDES GRILLES MAY BE CONNECTED TO ADJOINING ROOM

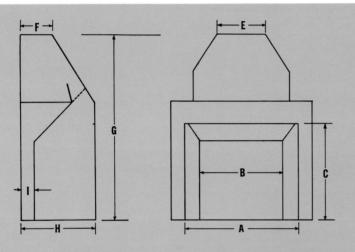

BASIC CIRCULATOR DIMENSIONS

For your general planning, the data below include useful inside and outside Circulator dimensions.

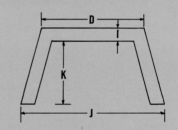

Model No.	Average Room Cap. (cu. ft.)	Fireplace Finished Opening		FLUE SIZES				Modular Flue Sizes, Rectangular	GENERAL DIMENSIONS OF CIRCULATOR										
		Wide	High	Chimneys Over 20'		Chimneys Under 20'			A	B	C	D	E	F	G	H	I	J	K
				Rect.	Rd.	Rect.	Rd.												
R2800	3520	28″	22″	8½″ x 13″	10″	8½″ x 13″	10″	12″ x 12″	28″	20″	22″	25″	12″	8″	44″	18¼″	3″	34¾″	15″
R3200	3850	32″	24″	8½″ x 13″	12″	8½″ x 13″	12″	12″ x 12″	32″	23″	24″	28½″	12″	8″	47½″	19¼″	3″	38½″	16″
R3600	4565	36″	25″	13″ x 13″	12″	13″ x 13″	12″	12″ x 16″	36″	27″	25″	32″	12″	12″	51½″	20½″	3″	43″	17″
R4000	4950	40″	27″	13″ x 13″	12″	13″ x 13″	12″	12″ x 16″	40″	30½″	27″	36½″	12″	12″	55″	20¾″	3½″	47¾″	17″
R4600	5720	46″	29″	13″ x 13″	12″	13″ x 18″	15″	16″ x 20″	46″	36″	29″	42½″	17″	12″	60″	22½″	4″	55″	18″
R5400	7040	54″	31″	13″ x 18″	15″	13″ x 18″	15″	16″ x 20″	54″	43¼″	31″	50½″	17″	12″	65″	23½″	4″	62½″	19″

accessories —

The following accessories aid in correct, satisfactory installation of the Circulator:

Heavy gauge formed steel lintel for positioning of masonry above firebox opening. Five sizes.

Grilles for placement at cold air intake and warm air outlet openings. Four grilles used in each Circulator installation.

Fans for adding forced air operation to the Circulator. Sizes for each of three different grilles.

Ash Dump of heavy formed steel or cast iron. Replaces one firebrick in hearth. Empties to ash pit below.

Steel or cast iron cleanout and ash pit doors for access to, and cleaning of, ash pit below hearth. Five sizes.

First, a dimensional plan should be provided by your mason, builder or architect and the proper size Circulator ordered.

Pour footing and foundation according to the dimensions in the plan (the chart on Page 76 gives minimum dimensions and may not include all non-combustible materials used to cover the fireplace). Gage thickness of footing by local conditions; consult local building code.

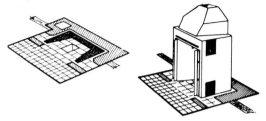

Lay firebrick on hearth area, including ash dump if one is to be used.

Set Circulator in position over firebrick area.

Consult detailed instructions for installing ash pit. This is not absolutely essential but should be installed for convenience of ash removal and to provide a place for installing a ventilating brick to admit combustion air.

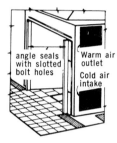

The instructions furnished are for common brick, 8″ x 4″ x 2¼″. They include special pointers for type of installation: slab floor, basement, multiple installations, etc. Notice that adjustable angle seals at sides provide a starting place for masonry.

Start brickwork, first setting return air boxes in place at hearth level. Lay hearth firebrick under Circulator only. Put in ash dump if one is to be used.

Set Circulator in position on hearth. Angle Seals are provided and must be metal-screwed to sides of fireplace opening.

Fiber glass wool is provided and must cover all outside surfaces of Circulator. Masonry must not come closer than ½″ to ¾″ to Circulator and must support itself. Thin layer of mortar will hold Fiber glass wool in place on unit.

Set lintel plumb. Place fiber glass between lintel and front of Circulator before laying bricks across lintel.

Return air and warm air outlet openings must be provided on each Circulator. Air must circulate through fireplace casing.

Locate air intake openings at sides or in front as required for your plan. Warm air outlets may be placed above or below mantel.

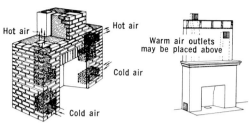

Plumb angle seals, tighten screws, and lay brick against them as a starting point. Set brick until most fiber glass is covered. Separate masonry air passages must be made between each set of return air and warm air boxes. If fans are used for forced air, wiring must be brought into both return air passages.

Upper part of fiber glass and warm air boxes are placed in the same manner and brickwork completed. Place generous amounts of fiber glass between lintel and Circulator front. Leave ½″ or more between top of Circulator and flue tile.

Schematic assembly below shows ash pit, hearth and Circulator. A capped chimney is also shown. (Notice one flue extends 6″ to 8″ above the other when more than one flue is built into a single chimney.)

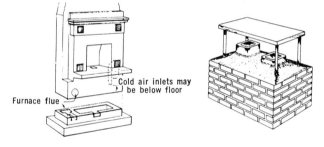

Chimney construction should follow the general rules given elsewhere in this book.

some circulator installation ideas—

The basic Circulator unit is the heart of a masonry fireplace installation with all the guesswork of proper proportioning for efficient operation eliminated. And, even though masonry is used to build this heating-type fireplace, any style of mantel or finish trim material may be used to personify your design taste and talents.

the multi-opening fireplace

The universal smoke dome — combining damper, lintel and smoke chamber in one integral unit — is used in the construction of multi-opening fireplaces.

To many, the "see-through" fireplace — open on two or more sides — has special appeal. History agrees, for ever since early man placed his fire in the midst of family and tribal activities, the centrally located fire has held this practical and socially significant position. Witness, as further examples, the campfire and the bonfire rally!

In the modern home, especially when guests are present, the fireplace viewable from several sides assumes an added charm; therefore, architects of custom homes have used the multi-opening fireplace increasingly in their attempts to "create something new and different." Actually, their achievements are modern adaptations of an idea nearly as old as fire.

With extra appeal, however, come additional construction and design problems. The additional open areas of this type of fireplace tend to create cross drafts which are both hazardous and detrimental to efficient operation. These can be counteracted only by creating a more powerful draft up the flue, and this additional vertical draft is brought about by increasing the size of the throat and flue area!

An answer to this problem was found some years ago in the Majestic Universal Smoke Dome, an integral dome and damper designed with deep, smooth-sloping sides and a large interior capacity which traps the smoke and funnels it toward the flue. (More on Pages 84-86.)

Variations of the Multi-Opening Fireplace

IN A CORNER

OPEN ALL AROUND

OPEN IN TWO ROOMS

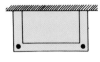

OPEN ON THREE SIDES

FRONT VIEW

SIDE VIEW

a few installation ideas —

more ideas for multi-opening fireplaces

In these scenes we can begin to appreciate the *special appeal* of the Multi-Opening, or "see-through," fireplace. Your own taste and imagination, plus a properly installed Majestic smoke dome, can make that dream fireplace a reality.

the majestic universal smoke dome

This integral unit, containing damper, smoke chamber and lintel, is the practical answer to multi-opening fireplace construction. The deep, smooth-sloping sides of the dome assure good draft while permitting unobstructed "see-through" design. Some general thoughts on installation follow:

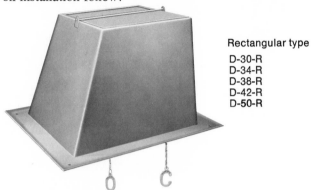

Rectangular type
D-30-R
D-34-R
D-38-R
D-42-R
D-50-R

Model No.	Rated Size		Top Outlet		Overall Size		
	A	B	E	F	H	L	W
D-30-R	30	16	12	17	17	37	23
D-34-R	34	20	17	17	17	41	27
D-38-R	38	20	17	17	25	45	27
D-42-R	42	20	17	23	25	49	27
D-50-R	50	24	21	23	28	57	31

Note: Lintel width on all models is 3½".

Flue Size

The flue size for the ordinary fireplace, enclosed on three sides, can be estimated by rule-of-thumb methods as an area proportionate to the size of the fireplace opening. However, cross drafts and other problems encountered in multi-opening fireplaces must be overcome by a stronger draft, and therefore larger flues are required. Since the fireplace opening size can vary not only vertically and horizontally, as in a single opening, but also by the number of sides open (two, three, four, or a complete circle), the flue must vary in proportion. Suggested flue sizes for different styles of fireplaces are given on Pages 85 and 86.

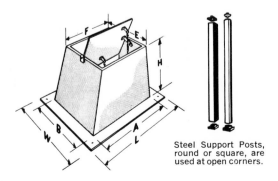

Steel Support Posts, round or square, are used at open corners.

General

Inspect the damper, making sure the valve plate is undamaged and free to operate. Check to see that the pull chains are securely fastened to the valve, with the "C" pull hanging from the side that opens above the damper body and the "O" from the valve side that opens down into the dome. Test the tension adjusting bolt (see diagram below) and re-adjust if necessary for proper operation. Tighten the nut against the tension arm to hold the tension bolt in the set position.

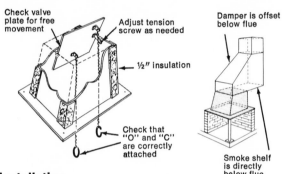

Check valve plate for free movement

Adjust tension screw as needed

½" insulation

Damper is offset below flue

Check that "O" and "C" are correctly attached

Smoke shelf is directly below flue.

Installation

Lay up the fireplace according to your plans until the desired opening height is reached (see specifications). The dome is now set in place, taking advantage of any built-up masonry sides as supporting ledges for the built-on damper flanges. Any projecting corner should be supported by a suitable post of adequate strength. With the damper perfectly level, accurately measure and cut the post to the length needed and set in place. Now pad the corners of the damper body with the ½" glass wool provided, and continue laying up the masonry. Keep bricks and mortar at least ½" away from the damper to allow for expansion and contraction of the metal.

Smoke Shelf

The flue tile should never be set directly above the damper opening but should be offset to one side. A smoke shelf, horizontal with the top of the damper, should be provided to impede and deflect downdrafts. It should be located directly beneath the flue tile, on any of the four sides of the damper. Actually, eight positions for the shelf (and the chimney above it) are available, since the damper can be reversed. The smoke chamber above the damper and the shelf should be generous in size, high enough so as not to impede the movement of the damper valve, and should be corbelled steeply to meet the bottom of the flue lining. For a smooth surface and better draft, the walls should be given a coat of cement mortar. From this point on, the mason should follow the best recommended practices for good chimney construction.

tables of opening heights and flue sizes—

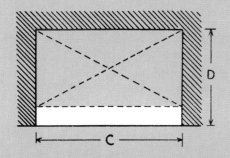

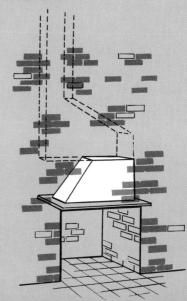

Type 1—Open One Side

For most fireplaces of this type, a Majestic steel throat damper serves efficiently. However, in cases of unusually high or deep fireboxes, Majestic's Universal Smoke Dome is the best answer. Smoke shelf may be built to right or left. (Tables on these pages are based on chimney height of 20′ measured from hearth to top of flue. Reduce opening heights 1″ for each 2′ drop in chimney height.)

Damper No.	Hearth Size		Maximum Opening Height For Sandard Flue Tile			
	C	D	8½x13	13x13	13x18	18x18
D-30-R	30	20	32	42	52	—
D-34-R	34	24	30	38	48	—
D-38-R	38	24	28	36	46	56
D-42-R	42	24	26	34	44	54
D-50-R	50	28	22	30	38	46

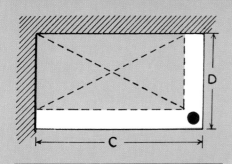

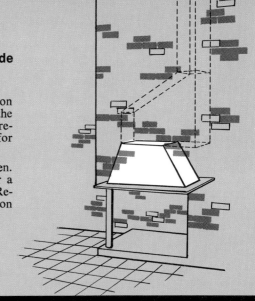

Type 2—Open One Side and One End

By far the most common and most popular of the modern, specialized fireplaces, ideally suited for Majestic Smoke Domes.

Sketch shows left end open. Reverse drawing for a right-end installation. Requires one post support on the projecting corner.

Damper No.	Hearth Size		Maximum Opening Height For Sandard Flue Tile			
	C	D	13x13	13x18	18x18	20x24
D-30-R	34	20	30	38	48	—
D-34-R	38	24	26	34	44	54
D-38-R	42	24	24	34	42	48
D-42-R	46	24	24	32	40	48
D-50-R	54	28	20	28	36	44

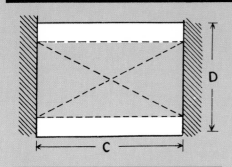

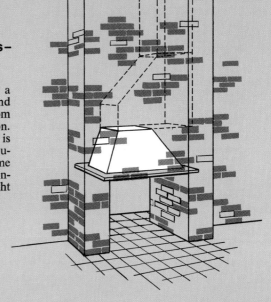

Type 3—Open 2 Sides— Ends Closed

Often used to provide a living room fireplace and a kitchen or family room barbecue in combination. This type of fireplace is rapidly increasing in popularity in the modern home as a room divider. Construct smoke shelf to right or left.

Damper No.	Hearth Size		Maximum Opening Height For Sandard Flue Tile				
	C	D	13x13	13x18	18x18	18x24	24x24
D-30-R	30	24	24	32	42	—	—
D-34-R	34	28	22	30	38	46	—
D-38-R	38	28	20	28	36	42	—
D-42-R	42	28	—	26	34	40	48
D-50-R	50	32	—	22	30	36	42

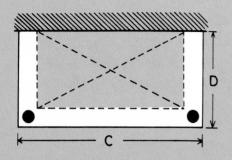

Damper No.	Hearth Size		Maximum Opening Height For Sandard Flue Tile				
	C	D	13x13	13x18	18x18	18x24	24x24
D-30-R	38	20	22	30	38	—	—
D-34-R	42	24	20	27	35	41	—
D-38-R	46	24	—	25	33	39	—
D-42-R	50	24	—	24	32	38	44
D-50-R	58	24	—	21	28	34	40

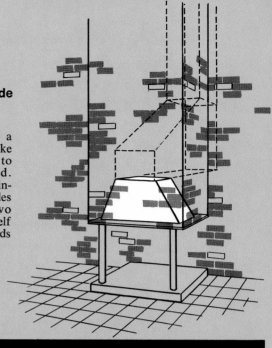

Type 4–Open One Side and Both Ends

Generally centered on a wall. Use a Majestic Smoke Dome, corresponding to size of hearth desired. Opening height may be increased by recessing sides into wall. Requires two corner posts. Smoke shelf should always be towards wall, or on slope end.

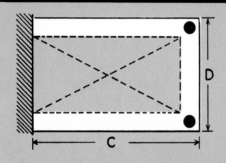

Damper No.	Hearth Size		Maximum Opening Height For Sandard Flue Tile				
	C	D	13x13	13x18	18x18	18x24	24x24
D-30-R	34	24	20	26	34	—	—
D-34-R	38	28	—	22	30	36	—
D-38-R	42	28	—	—	29	35	—
D-42-R	46	28	—	—	28	34	40
D-50-R	58	32	—	—	24	30	36

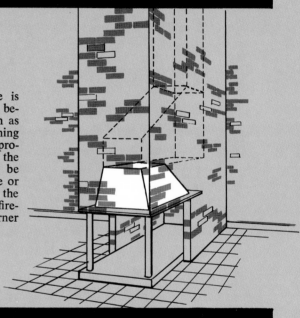

Type 5–Open Both Sides and One End

This type of fireplace is often used as a divider between two rooms, such as a living room and dining area. As in Type 4, a proportionate increase in the opening height may be made by extending one or both side walls, giving the effect of recessing the fireplace. Requires two corner posts.

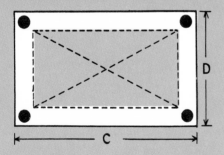

Damper No.	Hearth Size		Maximum Opening Height For Sandard Flue Tile				
	C	D	13x13	13x18	18x18	20x24	24x24
D-30-R	38	24	—	22	30	—	—
D-34-R	42	28	—	20	28	32	—
D-38-R	46	28	—	—	26	31	—
D-42-R	48	28	—	—	24	30	35
D-50-R	58	32	—	—	21	27	32

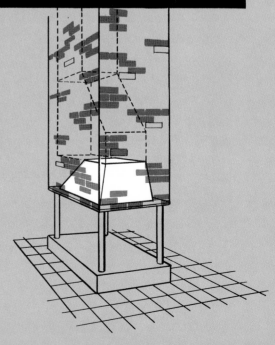

Type 6–Open Both Sides and Both Ends

Although basically the most primitive type of fireplace, this is also now the most "modern" and striking in appearance. Easy to construct using the Majestic Universal Smoke Dome Damper. Requires four extra heavy corner posts for supporting the total weight of masonry above.

enjoy charcoal cooking in your own fireplace the year 'round

Today, there is no need to limit the fun of open fire cooking to the out-of-doors and the balmy weather seasons. Small, portable, collapsible charcoal grills, such as the Majestic "Fire-B-Q", are designed for use in the indoor fireplace. The fireplace flue — with damper fully opened — provides an adequate outlet for charcoal smoke and cooking odors, and regular charcoal cooking may be enjoyed indoors on the most inclement days and evenings. In this way, home-owners get "dual-purpose" enjoyment from their fireplaces.

The "Fire-B-Q", measuring only 11⅛" high x 22" wide x 17" deep, stands in any average size fireplace when the fireplace is not in regular use. The 20" x 13" grill top is raised and lowered, to control cooking heat, by the use of a convenient crank handle. An adequate supply of charcoal fuel is held in the firebox below the grill top. The "Fire-B-Q" is readily collapsible and folds to a compact 4⅛" x 20" x 17" size for easy carrying to a picnic or other cooking site. The unit is finished in matte black enamel with chrome grill top, handle and legs.

acknowledgements

The material presented in this book is the culmination of years of fireplace specialization, experience and "know how" at The Majestic Company. Since 1907, Majestic has been involved in home heating and fireplace engineering and is a pioneer in the field of modern prefabricated fireplaces. This has included fireplaces for all fuels — wood, gas and electric — in both built-in and free-standing types. The Majestic Company proudly stands by its record of designing and manufacturing achievement in this field and believes that the information offered in FIREPLACE IDEAS is the most accurate available on the subject.

Inside Cover: **Walter Richardson, Architect.**   2: **James K. Levorsen, Architect.** 4: **House Beautiful.**   11 (upper left, lower left), 59 (bottom), 65 (top right), 81 (top), 83 (top right): **National Concrete Masonry Association.**   22: **Boat Deck, Inc.**   25 (top right), 28 (bottom right): **Project Development Corp.**   28 (top): **Sun Valley News Bureau.**   28 (bottom left): **Forest Pine Development.** 34: **House & Garden.**   35 (top left): **Good Housekeeping.**   35 (bottom): **Masonite Corp.**   42 (bottom right): **Patcraft Carpet.**   44 (middle left): **Southern Living.**   44 (bottom right): **California Redwood Association.**   56 (top left): **Western Wood Products Association.**   58: **West Coast Lumbermen's Association.**   59 (top): **Thomas Industries, Inc.**   64 (bottom left): **Marlite Wallpanels.** 65 (middle left): **National Lumber Manufacturers Association.**   67 (top right), 68 (top left), 68 (bottom left): **Cabin Crafts, Inc.**   67 (top left), 68 (bottom right): **Structural Clay Products Institute.**   67 (bottom right): **Armstrong Cork Company.**   67 (bottom left) **Simpson Timber Company.**   68 (top right): **Kentile, Inc.**   69 (top left): **National Oak Flooring Manufacturers Association.**   69 (bottom left): **Tile Council of America.**   69 (bottom right): **Southern Pine Association.**   82 (bottom): **Henry L. Newhouse, Architect.**   83 (top left): **Ceramic Tile Institute.**

An American-Standard Company

The Majestic Company, Huntington, Indiana 46750